Contents

Any words appearing in the text in bold, **like this**, are explained in the glossary.

A plant may be called different things in different countries, so every type of plant has a Latin name that can be recognized anywhere in the world. Latin names are made of two words – the first is the genus (general group) a plant belongs to and the second is its species (specific) name. Latin plant names are given in brackets throughout this book.

What is reproduction?

Every living thing on Earth, from the smallest insect to the largest tree, is here because of **reproduction**. Reproduction is the way plants and animals produce young that grow into new plants and animals that look like themselves. In the animal kingdom, cats produce kittens that grow into adult cats, and frogs produce eggs that hatch into tadpoles, which grow into frogs. In the plant kingdom, oak trees produce acorns that grow into new oak trees and potato plants produce potatoes that grow into new potato plants.

Why do plants reproduce?

All **organisms** (living things) gradually become older and eventually die. Some plants, like the poppy, live only for a few months. Others, like the yew tree, can live for thousands of years. If these plants did not reproduce and make other living things like themselves before they died, their **species** (kind) would die out.

◄ The ancestors of these horsetail plants were the giant horsetails that first grew on Earth nearly 400 million years ago.

Plant Reproduction

Richard & Louise Spilsbury

Heinemann
LIBRARY

www.heinemann.co.uk

Visit our website to find out more information about **Heinemann Library** books.

To order:
☎ Phone 44 (0) 1865 888066
🖷 Send a fax to 44 (0) 1865 314091
💻 Visit the Heinemann Bookshop at www.heinemann.co.uk to browse our catalogue and order online.

First published in Great Britain by Heinemann Library,

Halley Court, Jordan Hill, Oxford OX2 8EJ, part of Harcourt Education

Heinemann is a registered trademark of Harcourt Education Ltd.

© Harcourt Education Ltd 2002
First published in paperback 2003
The moral right of the proprietor has been asserted.

Designed by Macwiz
Illustrations by Jeff Edwards
Originated by Ambassador Litho Ltd
Printed in China by Wing King Tong

ISBN 0 431 11882 5 (hardback)
06 05 04 03
10 9 8 7 6 5 4 3 2

ISBN 0 431 11889 2
07 06 05 04 03
10 9 8 7 6 5 4 3 2 1

British Library Cataloguing in Publication Data

Spilsbury, Louise
    Plant reproduction. – (Life of plants)
    1.Plants – Reproduction – Juvenile literature
    I.Title II.Spilsbury, Richard, 1963–
    571.8'2

Acknowledgements

The Publishers would like to thank the following for permission to reproduce photographs:
FLPA: pp7, 13, 19, 24, 32; Holt Studios: pp4, 5, 6, 8, 10, 11, 15, 16, 17, 18, 21, 26, 28, 29, 36, 39;
Oxford Scientific Films: 9, 12, 14, 22, 25, 27, 30, 31, 33, 34, 37, 38; Science Photo Library: Adrienne Hart-Davis p23

Cover photograph reproduced with permission of Holt Studios.

Our thanks to Andrew Solway for his comments in the preparation of this book.

Every effort has been made to contact copyright holders of any material reproduced in this book. Any omissions will be rectified in subsequent printings if notice is given to the Publisher.

Kinds of reproduction

Plants use two main kinds of reproduction – **sexual reproduction** and **asexual reproduction**. In sexual reproduction a young plant has two parent plants. Plants that reproduce in this way, such as sunflowers and oak trees, make **seeds**. The seeds can then grow into new plants. When these young plants are fully grown, they will produce seeds that will, in turn, grow into new plants themselves. The majority of plants in the world make new plants using sexual reproduction.

Some plants, such as strawberry and potato plants, use asexual reproduction as well or instead of sexual reproduction. Asexual reproduction involves only one parent plant. One way of reproducing asexually is when a small part of the parent plant, such as a bit of **root** or **stem**, grows into a new plant. When this new plant is big enough, it breaks away from the parent plant and becomes a separate individual, able to live and reproduce new young plants of its own. Some plants, such as ferns, reproduce asexually using **spores**.

▲ These **saplings** have grown from seeds that dropped from the trees above.

Sexual reproduction in plants

Let's start at the very beginning, before a **seed** is even fully formed. A seed starts life, as all **organisms** do, as a tiny living part called a **cell**. Cells are the tiny building blocks that make up all living things. Plants, like many other organisms, have many different types of cells in the different parts of their bodies. For example, some cells are specialized to carry water around the plant, while others are specialized to make food by **photosynthesis**. The cells required for **sexual reproduction** are called **sex cells**, and organisms make these in their sexual (male or female) parts.

How does it work?

In the first stage of sexual reproduction, a sex cell from the male parts of an organism and a sex cell from the female parts of another organism have to fuse (join together). The new cell then divides many times and increases in number to make an **embryo**, a very early form of the new living thing. In plants, the embryo develops inside a **seed**. The seed forms inside the female parts of a plant. When the seeds are fully formed, the plant lets them go.

◄ These are the seeds growing at the top of wheat plants. People grow wheat for its seeds, which can be made into food such as bread.

Making a difference

Why do so many plants bother making seeds when they could simply split off a part of themselves to create a new plant? It is all to do with being different.

Inside each sex cell there is a special package containing information called **genes**. Genes are like tiny instruction manuals. They control not only how an organism looks but also how it will survive, grow and change through its life. When two sex cells fuse, they mix together two lots of genes, one from each parent. So, the embryo ends up with its own unique mixture of genes. It is rather like a recipe where you mix two ingredients together to create something different.

When a plant grows from a seed, it will be similar to its parent plants, but it will also be slightly different from both of them. These tiny differences may improve its chances of survival. When a plant makes a new plant from a part of itself, however, the new plant has the same genes and is exactly the same as its parent. This new plant will be no better at growing and surviving than its parent.

▶ **This poppy grew from a seed. It looks almost identical to its parent plants, but it may have subtle differences in its genes that help it to survive and thrive better than its parents.**

What flowers do

Flowers are the special parts of a plant where **seeds** are made. When you look at most flowers, the parts that catch your eye are the colourful and often large **petals**. You have to look more closely to see the parts that do the real work – they are tucked away in the centre of the flower. Here there are female and male parts that produce seeds that can grow into new plants.

Female part

The female part is usually found in the very centre of the flower. It is called the **carpel**. The carpel consists of three parts – the **ovary**, **style** and **stigma**. The ovary is the swollen or rounded part at the bottom of the carpel. This is where the seeds are produced. The ovary contains one or more female **sex cells** called **ovules**. The ovules are the bits that can develop into seeds. The stigma is at the top of the carpel. It has a pointed or flattened end which is usually sticky. The style is a single large stalk that attaches the ovary to the stigma.

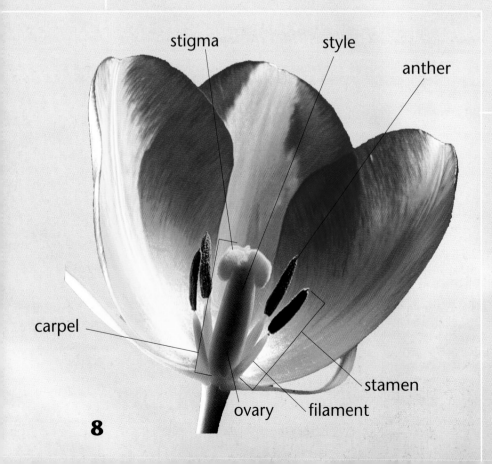

stigma

style

anther

carpel

ovary

filament

stamen

◄ **This photo of the centre of a tulip shows the male and female parts of the flower.**

Male part

The male part of a flower is called the **stamen**. Each stamen is made up of an **anther** and a **filament**. The anther is the enlarged tip of the stamen. It is like a special bag that produces and holds **pollen** grains. Pollen grains contain the plant's male sex cells. The filament is the part that supports (holds up) the anther. Some types of flowers have a few stamens, while others have many.

Different kinds of flowers

Most flowering plants make flowers that contain both male and female parts, as on the tulip shown opposite. Some plants make two different flowers – some with only female parts, others with only male parts. In some plants, such as oak (*Quercus*) and hazel (*Corylus*), both male and female flowers appear on the same plant. In other kinds, such as holly and fig trees, a single plant has either all male or all female flowers.

The secret of pollen grains

Pollen grains are so tiny – usually the size of bits of dust – that we never really see what individual grains look like. The only way to see a pollen grain is with the help of a microscope, which enlarges the image many times. Up close, you can see that each type of plant has its own individual kind of pollen grain – they may look like doughnuts, coffee beans, spiky balls or sponges, and some even have hairs on them!

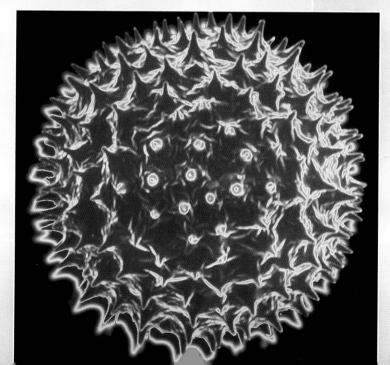

◄ This is a pollen grain from a mallow plant.

What is pollination?

Pollination is the first stage in the process of **seed** production. Before an **ovule** can become a seed, it has to join with the **pollen** of the same or another flower. Pollination is when pollen travels from the **stamens** (male parts) to the **carpels** (female parts) of the same plant or a different plant of the same kind.

Pollen clues

Pollen grains are very hardy, so they don't get damaged as they move from one flower to another. They are so tough that they can survive for many years. Scientists have used pollen grains preserved in marshy ground called **peat bogs** to work out what plants were growing on Earth thousands of years ago.

Pollen grains are produced in the **anthers** at the top of the stamen. When a plant's pollen is ready, the anthers open by splitting down the middle. The two sides curl back to expose and release the pollen. So how does the pollen move? We all know that most plants are rooted to the ground. As they cannot move from place to place to pass on their pollen, they have other ways of doing it. The two main ways are by wind and by insects. We will look at these in more detail later in the book.

◄ The petals of the bottlebrush (*Callistemon*) plant are very small and pale – it is the long, bright red stamens that put on the real show. They give flowers the appearance of the kind of brushes used to clean bottles.

Cross-pollination

Most flowers are designed to disperse (scatter) pollen from one plant to another plant of the same kind. The pollen is moved from the male parts of one flower to the female parts of another flower on a separate plant. This is called cross-pollination. Seeds made by plants using cross-pollination contain **genes** from two parents. Remember, a mixture of genes means new plants will have some of the features of each parent, but also some unique features that might help them survive in places their parents could not.

Many plants have ways of making sure that only cross-pollination occurs. A willow tree (*Salix*) has either all female or all male flowers, and the stamens of flowers on a saxifrage (*Saxifraga*) plant die before the **stigmas** have developed. The plant can be pollinated only by the pollen from a separate plant.

Self-pollination

Many plants are also able to self-pollinate. This means that the pollen from the stamen of a flower reaches the stigma of the very same flower. Plants often use this do-it-yourself technique when their chances of cross-pollination are over. Honeysuckle (*Lonicera*) flowers, for example, have stigmas that are held away from the anthers so self-pollination is unlikely. But towards the end of the flowering period, if cross-pollination has not occurred, the stigma droops down amongst the anthers to self-pollinate.

▶ **At the end of their flowering time the stigmas on honeysuckle flowers droop down and take up their own pollen.**

anthers   stigma

Pollination in action

On spring and summer days you can usually see bees flying from one brightly coloured flower to the next. If you keep watching, you may notice that they tend to visit the same kinds of flowers, perhaps landing on one type after another. When you see this happening you are watching **pollination** in action!

Pollen deliveries

Bees, butterflies, flies and midges are like living delivery trucks for plants that use insects to pollinate their flowers. The **pollen** these plants produce is slightly stickier, rougher or larger than pollen made by plants that use wind for pollination. When an insect lands on one of their flowers, the sticky pollen grains attach themselves to the insect's body or legs. When the insect flies off, it carries the pollen load with it. When it lands on another flower, the pollen brushes off again. If it brushes off onto the **stigma** of this next flower, then pollination has been successful.

Insects visit the flowers to eat a sweet-tasting liquid called **nectar**, stored at the base of the **petals**. The position of the nectar source is important. To get to it, insects have to brush past the **anthers**, which is when pollen sticks to them.

▶ As the bee dines on this flower's nectar, pollen is showered onto its back from above. When it lands on the next flower, the pollen rubs off onto the stigma.

Pollen pantry

Some flowers that are insect-pollinated do not produce nectar. Instead, their pollen is a **nutritious** foodstuff for insects. The poppy flower has lots of **stamens** that form its distinctive black centre. These make plenty of pollen – its insect visitors eat some of it, and transfer some of it when they move to another flower.

Animal antics

In some countries birds and other animals help to pollinate plants as well. As hummingbirds reach their long beaks into hibiscus flowers to steal nectar, pollen brushes onto their head.

In North American deserts, birds pollinate the saguaro (*Cereus giganteus*), or giant cactus, during the day and bats do the night shift!

▶ **In Australia, the small honey possum lives entirely on nectar and pollen that it licks from flowers using its long tongue.**

Flower shapes

Most flower shapes are designed to ensure that insects can land easily on them and that insects always rub against the stamens when they visit. Some flowers, such as hydrangeas, grow closely together in groups called **clusters**. These form a landing platform that makes it easy for insects to call. Some flowers, like foxgloves (*Digitalis*), have petals that form tubes that insects have to crawl into for the pollen or nectar. Take a good look at flowers next time you are out and see if you can see how their shapes help them to be pollinated.

Attracting insect pollinators

How do insects know which flowers to visit and when? The answer is that flowers use their colourful **petals** and sweet scents to entice their **pollinators**. Their red, yellow, blue and purple flowers are like advertisements, telling their insect customers that they have **nectar** to offer. The petals produce their sweetest and strongest scents when the **pollen** is ready, as this is when they most need to attract the insects.

Some insects, such as bumblebees, butterflies and hoverflies, **pollinate** a range of different flowers. Other flowers are pollinated only by certain kinds of insects. For example, some flowers use midges and flies for pollination. Midges and flies usually feed on dead and rotting material, so sweet-smelling flowers do not attract them. Instead these plants have flowers that smell of rotting food.

▲ Eucera bee on an orchid.

Masters of disguise

To make sure the right insects pollinate them, eucera bee orchids have become experts at disguise! These plants grow flowers that look and smell like a female eucera bee. The disguise is so convincing that the male eucera bee is tricked into thinking it really is a female bee. When he lands on the flower, the pollen on **anthers** at the top of the flower rub off on his head. He flies off again, only to be attracted to another bee orchid. When he lands on the next flower, the pollen rubs off onto its **stigma** and pollination is complete.

Honeyguides

As well as using scent to attract pollinators, many flowers have petals with special markings to show the insects the way to the nectar. These are called **honeyguides**. These markings often take the form of bright lines, coloured differently from the rest of the petal so that they stand out. Some flowers have patterns of dots leading to the nectar source. These markings are a bit like the markings on an airport runway, guiding the insects into the correct landing position. On their way in to the nectar source, the insects will almost certainly brush past the plant's **stamens** and **carpels** and pick up or drop off pollen.

If you look closely at most flowers you should be able to see their honeyguides, though some are visible only in **ultraviolet** light, which insect eyes can see but we cannot.

▲ As well as petal patterns like these, in most flowers the scent gets stronger at the base of the petals. These things help to lead the insects to the centre of the flower – to the nectar and stigma and stamens.

Open for business?

New flowers open on a horse chestnut tree every day during the flowering season. If you look closely you will see that some have yellow lines on the petals. These guide the bees into the centre of the flower to find the nectar. When the nectar has run out, the lines turn red. This tells the bees when a flower has run out of nectar. It is a bit like a shop with a 'Sold Out' sign above the door!

Pollen dispersal by wind

When you brush past grass plants in summer you may have noticed the clouds of dust that blow off the plants. This dust is **pollen**. Plants that use the wind to help them **pollinate** their flowers include grasses and many trees and **shrubs**. Their pollen is small and light so it is easily blown from the **anthers** and carried away by the wind. The wind can carry pollen further than you might think – up to 4800 kilometres away from parent plants in some cases.

Wind pollination is a bit of a random process. Plants cannot be sure where the wind will carry their pollen. There is only the slightest chance that a pollen grain will reach a **stigma** of the right kind of plant. So wind-pollinated flowers make incredibly large amounts of pollen – just one birch catkin may hold five and a half million pollen grains. By releasing such vast amounts of pollen, wind-pollinated plants increase their chances of **reproducing**. However, much of the pollen will land on different types of plants or fall to the ground and go to waste.

◀ **The catkins that hang from the alder tree (*Alnus*) are its male flowers. On dry days, the wind blows millions of grains of pollen from the anthers. In spring, rivers that alder trees grow by are covered in wasted pollen.**

Plants that use wind for pollination do not need big, bright **petals** or a sweet smell to attract insects. They have small, dull-coloured and unscented flowers, which sometimes do not even look like flowers. The important thing about wind-pollinated flowers is that they grow where they can easily catch the breeze. Most have anthers that dangle from the ends of long stalks. Their stigmas are often large and feathery, rather like little brushes. This gives them a better chance of sweeping up the pollen as it blows past.

Hay fever

Most pollen is so tiny that it cannot be seen by the human eye. However, when it blows into the eyes, nose or throat of a person with hay fever, it can cause sneezing, sore eyes, bad headaches and a blocked or runny nose. Many people take medicine to control their hay fever and avoid walking in grassy fields in summertime.

Grass flowers grow at the end of long, flexible **stems**. The stems hold the grass flowers above other plants and they move with the wind so the pollen is blown off easily. Stalks of flowers grow from the tops of the stems. When the pollen is ripe, the anther grows so that it dangles outside the flower. The wind carries the pollen to the feathery stigmas of another grass plant.

◀ **Grass flowers don't have petals. They have green, leaf-like scales to protect their flower parts. These are couch grass flowers.**

When does pollination happen?

▲ Some wind-pollinated trees such as this willow (*Salix*) release pollen early in spring, before too many leaves cover the branches and stop the wind moving their pollen grains.

Plants do not grow flowers, or produce and release **pollen** throughout the whole year. It is essential that these things happen at the correct time. Plants use up a lot of their **energy** growing flowers, and if they missed out on **pollination** they would miss the chance to **reproduce**. It is vital that each plant produces and releases pollen when the time is right.

Seasons

Most wind- and insect-pollinated plants produce and release pollen in the spring and summer months. One of the simplest reasons for this is to avoid the harsh winter weather. Hard rains and severe cold can damage flowers and their pollen. Also, more insects are around in spring and summer, so this is when insect-pollinated plants have a better chance of being pollinated. For example, butterfly-pollinated plants grow flowers in summer as that is when butterflies appear.

Night callers

Some flowering plants are pollinated at night. Many, such as evening primrose (*Oenothera lamarckiana*), are pollinated by moths, which only come out in the dark. Evening primrose flowers give off their strongest, sweetest scent at night so that moths can find them easily. Many of the flowers that are pollinated at night are white or cream-coloured, because these colours show up better in the dark or twilight than other colours.

An open and shut case?

Most plants are pollinated during the day. Because of this, some open their flowers in the daytime, but close them at night. These plants are using their flower **petals** to protect their pollen at night. Crocus flowers open only when it is warm and sunny. That is when the insects that pollinate them are about. At night, they close up their petals to keep the pollen safe until the next day.

Some flowers, like the daisy, close their petals in bad weather. Rain and even morning dew can damage their pollen. They close their flowers so the water cannot gather on them. In a really bad spell of rain, they might keep their petals closed for days. Flowers whose petals hang down, such as the foxglove, are not in danger of water collecting inside them so they do not need to close their petals.

◄ Wood anemones close at night and open up when the warmth of the sun touches them again the next day.

Delaying tactics!

Some plants produce flowers gradually, with some flowers appearing later than others. This gives them more time to be successfully pollinated. For example, the rosebay willowherb (*Chamerion angustifolium*) grows flowers in a spike shape. The flowers at the bottom open first. Gradually other flowers open, with those at the top opening last. Bees visit the flowers lower down first, and work their way up day after day until all the flowers on the spike have died.

Fertilization

Once the **pollen** from one flower has landed on the **stigma** of another flower, it is time for the next stage in the process of **seed** production – **fertilization**. Fertilization in plants is when a male **sex cell** from a pollen grain and a female sex cell from an **ovule** join to make a seed. The ovules of a flower, you remember, are inside the **ovary**, the bottom part of the **carpel** (or female part) of the flower. The question is – how does pollen travel from the top of a sticky stigma on the outside of the carpel to the inside of the ovary?

Into the ovary

The answer is that the pollen itself does not! Instead, a tube grows down from the pollen grain into the carpel. This tube passes through the stigma and down to the ovary. Then the male sex cell from the pollen grain travels down the tube. In the ovary it joins with the ovule. The ovule has now been fertilized and can grow into a seed. In some plants, like the geranium, this whole process takes only a few hours. In others, such as some orchids, it may take a few months.

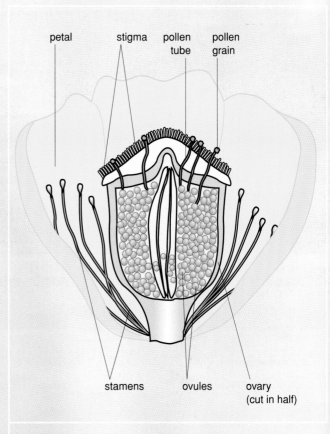

petal   stigma   pollen   pollen
                    tube   grain

stamens   ovules   ovary
                     (cut in half)

▲ **This picture shows a poppy ovary cut in half. Male sex cells from inside the pollen grains travel down to join with female sex cells in the ovules. Fertilization is then complete and the ovules can begin to develop into seeds.**

Pollen particulars

There is an important reason why each and every kind of flower in the world has its own unique brand of pollen. It means that pollen from one plant can only fertilize flowers from the same kind of plant. Only pollen from a flower of the same **species** can grow a tube down into the carpel of another flower. Poppy pollen cannot fertilize a buttercup, honeysuckle or lily flower. Pollen from the **anther** of a poppy flower can only enter the carpel and fertilize the ovule of another poppy flower.

What happens next?

After fertilization, the flower is no longer needed. Almost all the parts of the flower, including the **stamens** and usually the stigma and **style**, wither away. The flower **petals** fade and die and fall from the plant. The hollow part at the bottom of the flower – the ovary – is all that remains. It slowly forms a **fruit** to protect the seeds, which are growing inside.

▲ The red berries on this rose bush are called rosehips. They were once the ovaries of the rose flower. They have become bigger to protect the growing seeds inside.

21

Conifers

Many trees **reproduce** using flowers, just like other flowering plants. However, some trees, called **conifers**, reproduce using **cones**. Most conifers are **evergreen**, with needle-like leaves. Conifer trees include firs, cypresses, pines, cedars and redwoods.

Male and female cones

Conifers grow two kinds of cones – male and female. The male cone is the smaller and softer of the two. Male cones sometimes look like small **buds** or flowers and are often brightly coloured in shades of yellow, purple or red. When people talk about cones they usually mean the female ones. When fully grown these are much bigger than the male cones and have woody scales.

Male cones usually grow at the tips of branches, where their **pollen** can be caught by the wind. In spring, male cones release vast amounts of yellowish pollen. Most falls to the ground, but some lands on female cones of the same kind of tree. Female cones have two **ovules** on each of their scales with a tiny sticky patch close by. If a pollen grain sticks to this patch it can form a tube to reach into the ovule. Then the male **sex cell** from the pollen can join with the female sex cell in the ovule to form a **seed**.

◄ The female cones on the European larch (*Larix decidua*) tree are purplish red at first, becoming hard and woody as the seeds form. Male larch cones are smaller and yellow.

Male cones shrivel and die after they have released their pollen. Female cones grow larger when **pollinated**. Seeds take between one and three years to develop fully. They grow tucked between the scales of the female cones. At first many female cones are green and the scales are closed up tight to protect the young seeds. They turn brown and grow bigger and harder as they get older and the seeds inside get bigger.

Releasing the seeds

In some conifers, the scales fall to the ground when the seeds inside are ripe. The seeds are released as the scales fall. Many have papery wings to help them float in the wind and be carried far from the parent tree. Cedar cones form a stack of scales that fall off gradually. This ensures that at least some of the seeds fall when the conditions are right for **germination**. In pine trees, the scales open up and the seeds are blown away. Once all the seeds have been released, the cones fall to the ground.

▶ Pine kernels (which we sometimes call pine **nuts**) are actually the seeds from inside the cone of the stone pine tree (*Pinus pinea*). The stone pine seeds are quite big compared to other cone seeds and they have a tough outer shell to protect them.

Seeds

Most of the world's plant **seeds** are no bigger than a grain of sand. Yet inside these tiny capsules there is everything a new plant needs to start growing. The giant redwood tree (*Sequoiadendron giganteum*), which towers 80 metres above the ground, started life as a tiny seed, barely 2 millimetres long.

Inside a seed

A seed is like a **fertilized** egg. Inside there are two parts – a food store and an **embryo**. An embryo is like a baby plant. It has the new plant's tiny first leaves and **roots**. The food store will supply the young plant with the **energy** it needs to grow in the first days of its life. These inner parts of the seed are wrapped up in a protective **seed coat**. This keeps the seed safe until it is ready to **germinate** (start to grow). When a seed is released from its parent plant it may be some time before the conditions are right for it to grow. For example, many seeds start to grow only when the temperature is warm enough or if there is enough water. The seed coat keeps the embryo inside the seed safe from damage and stops it drying out until it is ready to germinate.

◄ Seeds in the sandy earth of a dry desert may wait months or even years for rains to come so they can germinate.

Many small seeds

Different plants make different kinds and amounts of seeds. Many plants produce vast numbers of seeds, because only a few will manage to grow into new plants. In the tropical forests of Central and South America, trumpet trees can make 900,000 tiny seeds in a season. Even a large oak tree can produce about 50,000 acorns in just one year. Imagine what would happen if all of these seeds grew into trees! In fact, most are eaten by animals or fall to places where they cannot grow. Even if they start to grow, many are soon eaten or trampled on and destroyed by hungry grazing animals. Only a small number survive long enough to celebrate their first birthday!

A few large seeds

Some plants produce a few large seeds instead of thousands of tiny ones. Big seeds, like the coconut, contain large food stores that help to make sure germination is successful. The food store gives the seed extra protection, so it has a good chance of surviving, germinating and growing into a new plant. However, if such a seed fails to germinate, the parent plant may well fail to **reproduce**.

▶ **A horse chestnut tree may produce hundreds of seeds – or conkers – each year. Only a few will germinate and grow into new trees.**

Seeds and fruits

A **fruit** is the part of a plant that develops from the **ovary** of a flower as a **fertilized ovule** ripens into a **seed**. It may take only weeks for the fertilized ovule to develop into a ripe seed. However, some seeds take much longer to grow – the seeds of **conifer** trees take up to three years to develop.

Fruits and the seeds inside them grow and develop at the same time. As the seeds get larger and riper, so do the fruits that hold them. When you see plums on a tree grow bigger and turn from hard and green to soft and purple, it is because the seed inside is gradually growing and ripening as well.

Fleshy and dry fruits

Many plants have fleshy fruits, such as plums and grapes. Some plants form dry fruits. Dry fruits include the pods of peas and beans, the hard shell of a hazelnut and the winged case of a sycamore seed. These have no thick flesh around their seeds.

▲ The flowers of the honesty (*Lunaria*) plant are not especially pretty. Gardeners choose this plant because of its unusual flat and transparent seed pods which look like pearly discs.

Seed dispersal

As well as protecting the seed as it grows, a plant's fruit has another equally important job to do. When the seed is ripe and ready to leave the parent plant it is the fruit that helps to carry it away. This movement of the seed away from the plant on which it grew is called seed dispersal. Different plants disperse their seeds in a variety of ways. The type of fruit that a plant produces depends on how the seeds are dispersed.

As children the best place for us to grow up is with our parents, or with other adults who care for us. The same is true for many young animals. Animal parents provide their young with shelter and food and keep them safe until they grow big enough to look after themselves. For plants, the opposite is the case. If seeds **germinate** too close to their parent plant they may not get the light they need to grow and their small **roots** will have to fight for space in soil already tangled with the roots of older, stronger plants. A seed's best chance of developing into a healthy new plant is to get far away from its parent plant before it germinates.

▶ A young **sapling** like this will not survive for long on a woodland floor as the light it needs to grow will be blocked by the leafy branches of the taller trees above.

Seed dispersal: wind and water

From plant to wardrobe!

The seeds of cotton bushes (*Gossypium hirsutum*) are carried in the wind by a tuft of white threads. These threads are so strong that people can spin them together to form the cotton thread used to make clothes such as jeans.

▼ When dandelion seeds land, the parachute breaks off and the seed sinks into the soil where it waits until it is time for it to **germinate**.

Flowering plants that use the wind to disperse (scatter) their **seeds** have special ways to make it successful. Poppies and orchids produce tiny seeds that are light enough to float on the wind when it shakes them out of their **fruits**. Some fruits also have special shapes to help them float or fly in the air before they drop to the ground. When these land, the fruits rot away and release the seeds into the soil.

Some plants, such as ash (*Fraxinus*) trees, have fruits that are shaped like wings, which enable them to twist away in the wind. Maple seeds grow in pairs and each pair is equipped with a wing-like blade. When the seeds are ripe the fruit falls from the tree, and the wings help them to spin like tiny helicopters in the air.

Some plants, such as dandelions and thistles, grow structures that work like miniature parachutes. Each tiny dandelion seed grows at the end of a thin stalk topped by a circle of white, wispy threads, which can be blown from the dandelion plant by even the gentlest of breezes.

Water works!

Plants that live near rivers, estuaries or the sea may use the moving water to scatter their seeds. Some of the seeds that use water dispersal are encased in fruits that have bubbles of air in them. These act like rubber rings, helping the fruits to float along on the surface of the water. The seeds of water lily plants may be dispersed over long distances in this way. They can germinate either in the water or, if they become stranded, on the shore or river bank.

◄ When a coconut washes up onto a beach, the outer husk rots away. The seed gets the **energy** and water it needs to germinate from the supplies it has carried inside it across the sea.

Coconut palm trees (*Cocos nucifera*) often grow on tropical beaches. Their green fruits contain the brown, hairy seeds that we buy in shops or win at fairgrounds! When the seeds are ripe, the fruit falls onto the beach and is washed into the water. The light husk around the coconut helps it to float. The white flesh inside the coconut is stored food and what we call coconut milk is really water. The coconut floats for sometimes thousands of kilometres across the waves, until it is washed up onto another beach. It may then germinate. This method of dispersal works so well that you can see coconut palm trees on beaches throughout the tropics.

Seed dispersal: fruit and nuts

Millions of animals all over the world help plants to disperse their **seeds**. But the animals involved are not even aware they are doing the plants a good turn – all they are interested in is making a meal of the **fruits** that the plants have produced.

When a bird picks a fruit such as a berry, it flies off to find a safe place to eat it. Sometimes it drops the berry while in flight; usually it eats the berry and spits out the seed. Either way, the bird has carried the seed a considerable distance and dropped it onto new ground, away from its parent plant. Some animals swallow the fruit and seeds together when they dine. The seeds' tough outer coat usually ensures that they survive being chewed and pass through the animal's body undamaged. When the seeds are expelled some hours and hopefully some kilometres later, they come out wrapped in their very own supply of **nutrients** – the animal's droppings.

The aardvark farmer

In the heat of the South African desert the aardvark gets its water from the juicy fruit of the gemsbok cucumber (*Acanthosicyos naudinianus*). This suits the cucumber plants perfectly as the aardvark has the habit of burying its dung (and the cucumber seeds) below the surface of the ground – out of the heat and at just the right depth for the seeds to **germinate**!

▶ **The fruit of the gemsbok cucumber is a favourite food of the aardvark.**

Ready when ripe

Have you ever wondered why fruits do not taste good until they are ripe? While the seed is still growing, fruits are often green, hard and sour to eat. Some fruits not only taste unpleasant when unripe, but they can also make an animal that eats them quite ill. Only when the seeds inside are fully developed, do the fruits ripen. Apples and cherries change from green to red and bananas turn yellow. The ripe fruits also give off a tempting scent, advertising to hungry animals all around that they are finally ready to eat.

Buried treasure – nuts and seeds

Hungry animals are also responsible for dispersing some of the seeds encased in dry fruits. Acorns hold the seeds of the oak tree. Animals such as squirrels collect and carry off many of these **nuts**. They eat some, but bury many others, often in open spaces, to return to in winter when food is scarce. However, squirrels, like many nut-hoarding animals, do not have perfect memories and many nuts are forgotten! In spring, when it is time to grow, many seeds find themselves in the perfect place for germination.

▶ **Acorn woodpeckers tuck acorns into specially drilled holes in tree bark as winter stores. Many seeds fall to the ground and germinate, or are stolen by rodents, who take them off and bury them in even more suitable spots!**

Other ways of dispersing seeds

Some plants do not rely on animals eating their **fruits** to disperse their **seeds**; they simply hitch a lift to get away. When you come back from an autumn walk in the country, take a look at your clothes. You might find that you are carrying hitchhiking fruits!

Some seeds have fruits covered in long hooks or lots of tiny spikes that stick to your clothes or to animal fur. You can pick them off with your fingers, but animals have to rub, scratch or lick them off. If these discarded seeds fall to the ground in a suitable spot, they may be able to **germinate**, well away from their parent plant.

Plant inventors

Did you know that when you do up your shoes or bag with a strip of Velcro™, you have a plant to thank for this useful device? A Swiss inventor called Georges de Mestral came up with the idea of Velcro™ after studying the way plant burrs stuck to his trousers. Take a close look at a piece of Velcro™ – it is made of many tiny hooks, just like the surface of a burr.

► Each of the fruits of the burdock plant (*Arctium minus*) is covered in tiny hooks. As an animal brushes past the plant, these cling to its fur and get a free ride to new ground.

Do it yourself!

Some plants are rather more independent. They do not need the help of wind, water or animals to scatter their seeds, because they are able to do the job of dispersal all by themselves. Some of these plants use a type of explosion to blast the seeds far and wide.

Many of the plants that have seeds in pods, such as pea and broom plants, release seeds in explosions. The pods of these plants are divided into two sections, which are closed tightly together as the seeds grow. When the seeds are ripe, the pods begin to dry out. In the heat of the sun they become drier and begin to twist and curl up until the two halves suddenly split open. The sudden blast fires the seeds off in all directions.

A vegetable rocket?

The Mediterranean squirting cucumber (*Ecballium elaterium*) uses a very special kind of explosion to discharge its seeds. As the seeds of this plant ripen, the cucumbers that hold them fill with slimy juice. The cucumbers get fatter and fuller until they suddenly shoot off their stalks into the sky, flying through the air like vegetable fireworks. As they travel, the juice and seeds spray from the fruits onto the ground below, where they may germinate.

Reproducing with spores

Many plants use **asexual reproduction** to produce offspring. Some of these reproduce using **spores**. Spores are tiny flecks of living material produced by a single plant. When released, the spores are able to grow into a new plant, identical to the parent plant. Plants that reproduce using spores include ferns and mosses.

Plants form spores in a number of ways. Moss spores are made at the tips of little stalks that grow above the leaves. In ferns, they are found on the underside of the leaves (or fronds), often seen as raised brown patches or spots. Some people mistakenly think these are a sign of disease. In fact, they are small sacs (parcels) of tiny spores.

When spores are ripe, spore sacs dry and split open, flinging the spores in all directions. The sacs usually open in warm, dry weather when the wind can more easily blow the light spores away. Spores may travel very long distances before the wind dies down and they fall to the ground far away from the parent plant. Only spores that land in the right conditions will be able to spring into life. Most spores need to land in damp, shady places in order to **germinate**.

◄ Spores that fall onto unsuitable ground will rot away, so mosses and ferns produce millions of spores to ensure that at least some land in places where they stand a chance of growing.

The three stages of fern growth

In many plants that reproduce using spores, such as ferns, there are three stages in the process of reproduction. The spore is the first stage. If a fern spore lands in a damp place, it grows into a thin, heart-shaped flap that looks like a tiny leaf. This is called a **prothallus**, and is the second stage. The prothallus looks nothing like the plant it came from, but a new fern will grow from it.

On the prothallus there are male and female parts. **Sex cells** from the male parts swim to the female parts of the same or a different prothallus. When a male and a female sex cell join, they begin to form a new fern plant. At first the baby fern grows on the prothallus. When the new plant grows its own leaves and **roots**, the prothallus dies. This new fern plant is the third and final stage.

A fern's development is a bit difficult to follow. It might be helpful to think of how a caterpillar turns into a chrysalis and a butterfly emerges from the chrysalis. In the same way, a spore turns into a prothallus and a fern plant emerges from the prothallus.

▶ **This fern *prothallus* is about the size of your smallest fingernail. It is the second stage in the life of a fern plant.**

Asexual reproduction in plants

Many plants are able to **reproduce** without **seeds** or **spores**. As well as making seeds, many flowering plants can also use another kind of reproduction to make new versions of themselves. Parts of these plants break off and grow into new, identical copies of their parent. This is called **asexual reproduction**.

Bad weather in spring or summer may prevent flowering plants from forming flowers or stop insect **pollinators** visiting them. This is not a problem if the plant can reproduce in other ways. There are disadvantages to asexual reproduction, however. Although some plants can make hundreds of seeds, they can make only a few new plants by producing **runners**, **tubers**, **bulbs** or **rhizomes**. Also, as they are identical copies, they may be no better than their parent at growing in the same **habitat**.

◄ Strawberries produce runners that result in identical copies of the parent plant.

The 43,000-year-old parent!

Some of the oldest plants in the world reproduce without the use of seeds. There is a **shrub** in Tasmania, Australia, that scientists believe comes from a parent plant that is more than 43,000 years old. King's holly (*Lomatia tasmanica*) spreads by producing new young plants that are clones (identical to itself). The original parent of this particular plant is long dead, but it lives on in the offspring that grow almost 1.5 kilometres wide and up to 8 metres tall.

Runners

Runners are long **stems** that grow sideways instead of upwards from a plant. They reach across the surface of the soil like skinny tentacles or fingers, searching out new ground. Strawberry plants grow runners. At intervals along the length of a runner, sets of new **roots** and **buds** start to grow and form tiny new strawberry plants. After a short time these new plants will be big and strong enough to survive by themselves. If the runner that attaches them to the parent plant dies or is damaged, the new plants keep on growing.

Buttercup plants (*Ranunculus acris*) also grow runners. They grow one new plant at the tip of a runner, and as soon as it is able to survive on its own the old runner withers away. Once the new buttercup plant is fully grown, it grows a runner of its own to produce one new buttercup plant.

The piggyback plant

Have you ever given a friend a piggyback ride? If you ever see a piggyback plant (*Tolmiea menziesii*) you might be fooled into thinking it got its name by giving other plants a ride. In fact this plant has a curious way of reproducing. Tiny new plants start to grow from the base of large, older leaves so it looks just as if they are having a piggyback ride!

Reproducing from underground

Some plants **reproduce** by growing new young plants from swollen underground parts. The underground parts are protected from harsh weather by the soil. They often remain unharmed for long periods until the conditions are right for them to grow into new plants.

Tubers and rhizomes

A **tuber** is an underground **stem** or **root** that the plant uses as a food store. The tuber becomes swollen with food as the plant above ground grows. When a dahlia's (*Dahlia*) flowers and leaves die in autumn, the plant lives on underground as a root tuber. In spring, it uses **energy** from the food stored in the tuber to grow new leaves and flowers. Potatoes (*Solanum tuberosum*) are also stem tubers. If you look at a potato you can see spots on it. These are **buds**, which we call 'eyes', and each one can grow into a new potato plant.

A **rhizome** is a special stem that grows sideways, at or just below the soil surface. Rhizomes produce leaves and flowers that rise above the soil, and small roots below. These can break free and become separate plants. Some plants also use rhizomes as a place to store food. Plants that grow rhizomes include iris (*Iris*), wild ginger (*Asarum canadense*) and bracken (*Pteridium aquilinum*).

◄ You can often see the rhizomes of iris plants protruding from the soil at the base of the plant's long, sword-shaped leaves.

► These are narcissi (left) and tulip (right) bulbs. These bulbs can produce flowers early in the year by using their stored food.

Bulbs

Bulbs are underground plant parts. They are made up of layers of thick, fleshy leaves growing around a central bud. Onions are bulbs, and lilies and tulips are flowers that grow from bulbs.

A bulb acts as a winter food store for the main plant but can grow completely new plants as well. New plants form from small buds that grow from the bulb's side. At first these buds are tiny, but as they get bigger they grow their own roots, leaves, stems and flowers. Eventually, the new bulb and its plant break away from the parent plant to form a separate individual.

Results of reproduction

In this book we have looked at the different ways in which plants reproduce. From **seeds** to **spores**, **runners** to rhizomes, the plants of the world use various methods of reproduction. Some plants use **asexual reproduction**, which involves only one parent plant. Others use **sexual reproduction**, which requires two parent plants. The methods may be different but when all plants reproduce they share a common aim – to ensure that they produce offspring that will live on after they have died.

Reproduction is a vital part of the life cycle of every plant. Only by reproducing can plants ensure that their **species** will survive and go on to produce future generations.

Try it yourself!

Try these experiments and activities to find out more about some of the plant processes you have learnt about in this book.

Fruit fun

Looking inside different kinds of **fruit** is a great way of understanding more about where and how **seeds** grow and what makes a fruit.

You will need:
- A selection of different fruits and **nuts** from the supermarket
- Paper and pencils
- A knife
- A chopping board
- A nutcracker

Ask an adult to help you slice one of each different kind of fruit in half on the chopping board. Lay them all out on a piece of paper. You should be very careful when opening the nuts in particular (you may need to use a nutcracker).

Make notes or draw a picture of each fruit to show how many seeds it has, where in the fruit they grow, and whether you think it is a fleshy or a hard fruit.

You could also take out the seeds and examine them. If you take their **seed coats** off you may be able to see inside the seeds.

Seed samplers

You can make displays with seeds that are nice to look at and that can help you learn about the different kinds.

You will need:
- A collection of seeds. (You can use some seeds taken from fruits, but you can also use seeds you can buy from the shops, such as sunflower, sesame and poppy seeds.)
- Glue
- Two sheets of thick paper

Lay out a design using groups of seeds onto one of the sheets of paper. You could make a scene, a portrait or an interesting pattern. When you are happy with it, cover the other piece of paper with glue and gradually transfer the seeds into position on the new piece of paper. Or you could try covering a piece of paper with glue and putting it onto your seed pattern to transfer it.

Identifying flower parts

The parts of a flower look different on different kinds of flowers. This activity will help you know what to look for.

You will need:
- Three different flowers, perhaps taken from a bunch from the supermarket
- Paper and pencils
- A knife
- A magnifying glass

Ask an adult to help you cut each of the flowers in half. Lay the flower halves out and see if you can work out what the different parts that you can see are. You could try writing labels on the paper behind the flower. Try to label **stigma, style, ovary, anther, filament, petal** and **stem**. With a magnifying glass you may also be able to see **pollen** on the anthers and the **ovules** inside the **ovaries**.

Spore prints

You have to wait until you find a fern frond (leaf) with brown **spore** sacs on the underside to do this activity, but it is very effective and worth the wait!

You will need:
- Fern fronds that have spore sacs growing on the underside
- Sheets of white paper
- A large, heavy book

Lay the fern fronds between two sheets of paper. Make sure the undersides of the leaves are facing downwards. Then place this paper 'sandwich' between the end pages (or underneath) the heavy book. Leave the book for a few days before opening the book and taking out the paper very carefully and keeping it the right way up. When you lift up the fern frond, you will find that the sacs have pressed into the paper leaving an interesting pattern in the shape of an outline of the fern frond.

Looking at plant reproduction

Different methods of seed dispersal

There are four main methods which plants use to disperse their **seeds** – wind, water, animal and explosion.

Wind-dispersal

Seeds dispersed by the wind tend to be very small and very light so they can be carried by a breeze when released from their **fruit**, or they have fruits with features that enable them to become airborne.

- *Lightweight seeds*: poppy, orchid
- *Seeds with winged cases*: sycamore, maple, linden, ash
- *Seeds with hairy or feathery fruits*: dandelion, cotton, clematis, artichoke, pussy willow, thistle

Water dispersal

Many aquatic plants use the water in which they live to disperse their seeds. Water-dispersed seeds need to be small and light enough to float, or have fruit with special features to help them stay on the surface of the water.

- *Small lightweight seeds*: alder, weeping willow.
- *Seeds with buoyant (able to float) fruits*: coconut, sea heart, lotus, prickly palm

Animal dispersal

Animals may eat soft fruit and any undigested seeds are passed out in their droppings. Animals store **nuts** that they forget. Other animal-dispersed seeds have fruits with hooks or prickles so that they catch on to the coats of passing animals and hitch a ride to a new spot.

- *Seeds with soft, edible fruits*: elderberry, blackberry, cherry, rosehip
- *Nuts that animals carry away*: acorns, sweet chestnut, hazelnut, Brazil nut, almond
- *Seeds with hooked or spiky fruits*: burdock, goosegrass, grapple hook

Explosion dispersal

Some fruits explode when the seeds inside are ripe to scatter the seeds away from the parent plant. Many dry up and shrink so they curl and split and spray the seeds around.

- *Examples include*: pea, broom, gorse, locust, runner bean

Pollen dispersal

All plants that produce **pollen** use wind, insects or other animals for **pollination**. Generally, the more drab the flower, the more likely it is a wind-pollinated plant. Animal-pollinated flowers are usually more colourful and scented.

Wind-pollinated plants
- Grasses
- Sedges and rushes
- Conifers, such as pine, spruce and fir
- Hazel
- Willow
- Poplar
- Walnut
- Oak
- Cedar
- Beet
- Corn
- Sagebrush
- Ragwood
- Russian thistle (tumbleweed)

Insect-pollinated plants
- Pansies
- Tulips
- Roses
- Gardenia
- Squash
- Cucumber
- Cabbages
- Foxgloves
- Apple trees
- Orange trees
- Water lilies
- Poppies
- Orchids
- Clover
- Honeysuckle

Other animal-pollinated plants
- Saguaro cactus (birds and bats)
- Hibiscus (hummingbirds)
- New Zealand flax (geckos)
- Eucalyptus (possum)
- Baobab (bat)

Different methods of reproduction

In this book we talked about the different ways in which plants **reproduce**. Here are lists of the different types of reproduction, with some examples of the plants that use each kind. Remember some plants may use more than one kind. Strawberries make seeds as well as reproducing by making **runners**.

Sexual reproduction *(seeds)*
- Poppies
- Oak trees
- Sunflower
- Sweet chestnut
- Rhododendron
- Flax
- Angelica
- Cherry
- Strawberry

Sexual reproduction *(cones)*
- Pine
- Spruce
- Fir
- Redwoods
- Cedars
- Cypresses

Asexual reproduction *(runners, tubers, rhizomes, bulbs)*
- *Bulbs*: Crocus, daffodil, tulip
- *Runners*: Strawberry, cinquefoil, white clover
- *Rhizomes*: Iris, bracken, ginger, goldenseal, licorice, valerian
- *Tubers*: Potato, dahlia, cassava

Asexual reproduction *(spores)*
- Ferns
- Mosses
- Liverworts
- Algae

Glossary

anther top part of the male part of a flower (stamen) where pollen is found in pollen sacs

asexual reproduction when a plant reproduces by creating another plant from a part of itself

bud swelling on a plant stem of tiny, young, overlapping leaves or petals and other parts of a flower, ready to burst into bloom

bulb underground bud protected by layers of thick, fleshy leaves. An onion is a kind of bulb.

carpel name for the female parts of a flower. The ovary, style and stigma together make up a carpel.

cells building blocks of living things, so small they can only be seen with a microscope. Some microbes consist of only a single cell, but most plants and animals are made up of millions or billions of cells.

cluster group of flowers growing together

cone form of dry fruit (in which seeds develop) produced by conifer trees. Cones are often egg-shaped and they are made up of lots of overlapping scales in which seeds grow.

conifer kind of tree that has cones and needle-like leaves

embryo a plant embryo is a very young plant contained in a seed

energy ability in living things to do what they need to do in order to live and grow. Plants and animals get the energy they need from their food.

evergreen type of plant that does not lose all its leaves at once, but loses some leaves and grows new ones all year round

fertilize/fertilization when a male sex cell and a female sex cell join together and begin to form a seed

filament part of a flower that holds up the anther

fruit part of a plant that contains and protects its seeds

genes inside each sex cell there is a special package containing information called genes. Genes control not only how an organism looks, but also how it will survive, grow and change through its life.

germinate/germination when a seed starts to grow

habitat place where plants (and animals) live

honeyguides special markings on flowers that lead insect pollinators to the nectar store. They are close by the flower's reproductive parts to ensure that the insect receives or delivers pollen.

nectar sugary substance plants make to attract insects, which like to eat it

nut kind of dry fruit. The hard shell of a nut is the fruit. The inner part, which we sometimes eat, is the seed.

nutrients kinds of chemicals that nourish plants and animals

nutritious healthy, full of nutrients

organism living thing, such as bacteria, cells, plants and animals

ovary rounded bottom part of the carpel. This is the part of the flower that may turn into a fruit containing the seeds.

ovule plant's female sex cell. Ovules are found inside the ovary and can become seeds after they have joined together with a male sex cell from a pollen grain.

peat bog area of marshy ground formed from the partly rotted remains of a plant called bog moss. Peat has proved to be an excellent preservative – things trapped inside peat can last a very long time without rotting away.

petals coloured parts of a flower

photosynthesis process by which plants make their own food using water, carbon dioxide (a gas in the air) and energy from sunlight

pollen tiny, dust-like particles produced by a flower, which contains the plant's male sex cells

pollinate/pollination when pollen travels from the anthers of one flower to the stigma of the same or a different flower

pollinator insect or animal that carries pollen from one flower to another and so helps plants to pollinate

prothallus tiny, plant-like organism that grows from a spore. A fern prothallus can produce a new fern plant.

reproduce/reproduction when a living thing produces young like itself

rhizome special kind of stem that grows under the ground instead of up in the air

roots plant parts that grow under the ground. These hold a plant in place and take in water and nutrients from the soil.

runner long, thin stem that grows sideways from a plant. New plants can grow from runners.

sapling young tree

seed seeds contain the beginnings of a new plant

seed coat tough, outer skin of a seed that protects the tiny, new plant inside that is waiting to grow

sex cell type of cell that plants and animals make in their sexual (male or female) parts. When a male sex cell and a female sex cell join, they can form a seed.

sexual reproduction when a plant reproduces by fusing a male and a female sex cell

shrub plant with a woody stem. The only real difference between trees and shrubs is their size. Tree-like plants that do not grow above 6 metres tall tend to be called shrubs.

species kind of living thing

spores tiny particles, usually containing a single cell, that are released by plants. Spores are resting cells that are good at surviving in difficult conditions, such as extreme cold. Once conditions improve, the spores grow and develop.

stamen part of a flower that produces pollen

stem part of a plant that holds it upright and supports its leaves and flowers

stigma part of the flower that receives pollen in the process of pollination. Stigmas are usually found at the top of a stalk, called the style.

style stalk which holds up the stigma of a flower and which attaches the stigma to the ovary

tuber short, thick underground stem. New tubers (and from those, new plants) can grow from the buds (called 'eyes') on a tuber.

ultraviolet kind of light that insects can see and we cannot

Find out more

Books

Eyewitness Guides: Plant and *Tree*, David Burnie, (1989 and 1988) Dorling Kindersley

Eyewitness Visual Dictionaries: Plants, Deni Brown, 1992, Dorling Kindersley

Internet-linked Library of Science: World of Plants, L. Howell and K. Rogers, 2001, Usborne; some of the website links can be reached via
www.usborne.com/quicklinks/quicklinks.asp

Plants, Jo Ellen Moore, 1986, Evan-Moor Educational Publishers

The Oxford Children's Encyclopedia of Plants and Animals, 2000, Oxford University Press

The Private Life of Plants, David Attenborough, 1995, BBC Books; also available as a set of videos of the BBC television series of the same name.

Websites

Great Plant Escape: fun way of learning about what different plant parts do; also a simple glossary of terms
www.urbanext.uiuc.edu/gpe/gpe.html

BBCi nature: gardening calendar, fun facts and links to Private Life of Plants information based on TV series presented by Sir David Attenborough
www.bbc.co.uk/nature/plants/

Alien explorer: looks at what plants are like and where they grow, from an outsider's point of view!
www.alienexplorer.com/ecology/topic27.html

Habitats of the world: at Missouri Botanical Garden's website, you can compare the habitats of the world
mbgnet.mobot.org/index.htm

Conservation sites

Information on dangers to wild plants and habitats and what conservation groups are doing to help them survive

Worldwide Fund for Nature
www.wwf.org.uk

Friends of the Earth
www.foe.co.uk/campaigns/biodiversity

Eden Project: lots of information about the remarkable Eden greenhouses, where different plant habitats have been created, plus an interesting plant quiz
www.edenproject.com/3772.htm

Places to visit

Many museums, arboretums (botanical gardens devoted to trees) and botanic gardens are fascinating places to visit. You could try:

The Royal Botanical Gardens, Kew, near London

Westonbirt Arboretum, Gloucestershire

Eden Project, St Austell, Cornwall

You can also find out about plants by visiting local garden centres.

Index